ARTIFICIAL INTELLIGENCE
THE PYTHON CHATBOT
IN AUSTRALIA

Yeeshtdevisingh Hosanee

Acknowledgement

Special thanks go to Mrs Suryamball Hosanee, the mother of the author, for her tremendous input during the whole publication process of this book. The author wishes to also thank her sister, Kedarshinisingh Hosanee, Dr Panchoo, Priya, Kavish, her friends and colleagues for their continuous encouragement in relation to the publication of this book. Special thanks to my publisher for the support in publishing this book.

Table of Contents

List of Figures

List of Tables

Introduction

Since 1956 till today, Artificial Intelligence (AI) as a concept, has been a fascinating field, mostly known to tech experts. Many AI books are of A4 size, with over 200 pages, which intimidate non-technical readers.

This small pocket-sized book is designed for readers new to the topic, aiming to help both technical and non-technical individuals, to follow along easily. It breaks down complex concepts using analogies and explains them in a stepwise approach. The steps can be reproduced by any readers and can be enhanced.

The aim of this book is to support readers to build an AI chatbot program. With this particular chatbot example, readers can build other types of AI projects. The AI chatbot program in this book, is a software application which allows users to input queries via text or voices. The AI chatbot can respond to each user's queries.

The programming language used in this book is the Python language. AI concepts such as Natural Language Processing (NLP), prediction's formula, computer vision and machine learning technique such as Euclidean distance have been used in this book.

A prior knowledge to programming concepts is not necessary. In Chapter 2 and 3, programming concepts are self-taught, with simple English and metaphorical language. Chapter 2 explains basic programming concepts, what we call the procedural programming paradigm and in Chapter 3, elicits the Object-Oriented Programming concepts, another programming paradigm.

Chapter 4 provides the aim of the AI chatbot. The chapter provides also an overview of the upcoming chapters. Chapter 5 to 14 provide detail description of the concept to be used to build an AI chatbot.

To familiarise the concept to Australian readers and invite curiosity to non-Australian readers, the examples taken in this book are related to Australia. For instance, in Chapter 9, to interact with the AI chatbot, the following three Australian museums have been used: *Melbourne Museum, Melbourne Maritime Museum and Melbourne Museum of Printing*

In Chapter 9, when a user entered the keywords "Melbourne" and "*Maritime*" using his/her computer keyboard, the AI chatbot recommended visiting the "*Melbourne Maritime*

Museum". Additionally, the chatbot provides the user with a biography of the museum.

In Chapter 10, when a user utilised a microphone to search for the keywords "*Melbourne*" and "*Printing*", the AI chatbot successfully recommended the "Melbourne Museum of Printing" based on searched keywords.

In chapter 11, when a user searched for the "*Adelaide*" location on a world map, the chatbot located the region on a Google Map (The Map is not illustrated in this book due to Photography copyright, but the Python codes are given to be reproduced by the reader).

In Chapters 12-14, users can ask the AI chatbot about the shortest travel distance among various regions. For instance, when a user inputted multiple destinations like "*Perth*," "*Sydney*," "*Ballarat*," and "*France*," and asked the AI chatbot for the shortest distance from "*Melbourne" (origin)*, the chatbot identified "*Ballarat*" as the closest destination. All these regions are mapped on Google Maps. The last chapter, which is Chapter 15, consists of the full codes for the AI chatbot application, which can be copied to reproduce the same AI chatbot.

Chapter 1: What is Artificial Intelligence?

1.1. What is Artificial Intelligence?

Intelligence is a word that is associated to the human mind or human brain. Artificial intelligence, AI, is the intelligence created for machines. A machine is an electronic device such as a computer, a laptop, a washing machine, a mobile phone, or an Automated Teller Machine (ATM).

Artificial Intelligence is a concept which allows machines to behave in a similar way to human beings. Decision making, prediction, forecasting and observing historical information are some examples of tasks which can be performed today by machines. These tasks do use a lot of the AI concepts.

1.2. Difference between AI and Computer Programming

An AI program or AI application, uses programming concepts, alike a standard program. However, an AI program differs from a standard program in their goals. When you build an AI program, you may need to work with extensive amount of data to either perform different kind of analysis or work with many mathematical models to perform a set of calculations.

For example, a dentist may need a standard software program to schedule appointments for his patients. Such program will require only basic programming concepts to be developed.

If the dentist now wishes to add other functionalities to his existing appointment program, he can extend the program with additional functionalities. For instance, if he wants to schedule appointments on the oncoming public holiday, the dentist's program will have to base itself on previous data of past appointments (historical data) to accurately provide the predicted number of appointments on the next public holiday. Such kind of functionality related to the observation of past historical data, will require the AI concepts and eventually make the extended appointment program an AI program.

Depending on your goals, you can determine the type of program you wish to build. Today, the types of program differ from standard or an AI program.

1.3. Psychology and Intelligence

In the world of psychology, Raymond B. Cattell has been credited for his theory about fluid and crystallized intelligence (Brown, 2016). The fluid intelligence is the ability to process new information, learn and solve problems. Whereas crystallized intelligence is your stored knowledge accumulated over the years.

The following table shows a comparison between the two types of intelligence:

Table 1 Fluid and crystallized differences

	Fluid Intelligence	Crystallized Intelligence
1.	Processes new Information in the brain	Processes Stored Information in the brain
2.	Short-Term memory	Long-term memory
3.	improves through childhood, peaks at adolescence, then declines	improves through childhood, and slows with aging, then stabilizes or continues to increase throughout life
4.	abilities include working memory, processing speed, reasoning, cognitive control, inhibition, complex skills, attention tasks, creativity	abilities include knowledge or wisdom.

The first difference in Table 1, shows that in fluid intelligence, the brain processes new information to store knowledge and in crystallized intelligence, the brain uses the stored information you have had from your previous experiences. For example, when you were a child and you learned alphabetical letters for the first time, it was new to you. The fact that it was new to you, and you did neither have any past experiences nor exposures to the alphabet, allowed you to develop the fluid intelligence in your brain at that time.

However, once you have been familiar with alphabetical letters, , you have the capacity to now group these individual letters together, to form words or group of words, in order to create different sentences. You can create these different groupings of letters because you know how to write the individual letter character (symbol). Hence, in this case you are building your crystallized intelligence when you are grouping letters to create either new words or new sentences from individual alphabetical letters.

The second difference shown in the previous table, is associated to your type of memory in the brain. There exist two types of memory: short-term and long-term memory. Fluid intelligence is associated with the short-term memory. With the capacity of your short-term memory, you are able to read and write alphabetical letters. Unfortunately, children with dyslexia and dysgraphia disorders, are not able to develop sufficient fluid reasoning skills because their short-term memory's capacity is low.

Once a person develops the fluid reasoning skills, he is encouraged to build his crystallized knowledge. To build this crystallized knowledge, one needs to keep practising reading and writing so that the same information in the short-term memory is moved onto the long-term memory in the brain. As, crystallized knowledge is associated to the long-term memory, in the brain, information needs to be moved to long-term memory to develop ongoing knowledge.

The third difference in table 1, is about the growth stages of the two types of knowledge. Fluid intelligence is developed from childhood, peaks during adolescence and then declines in adulthood, compared to crystallized knowledge, whereby the knowledge increases through childhood and does not decline, but instead slows down or stabilises or increases more.

The fourth differences of the two types of intelligence shown in the Table 1., are related to the cognitive skills they both build inside the brain. In fluid knowledge, skills such as reasoning, decision making, creativity are developed, which use the working memory to speed up reasoning skills and perform task faster. Whereas the crystallized knowledge, is not associated to the speed of processing, but rather in the quantity of knowledge you have acquired as a cluster in the brain, which can help to eventually gain wisdom.

1.4. Areas of Artificial Intelligence

Machine Learning, Deep Learning, Neural networks, Cognitive Computing, Natural Language Processing and Computer Vision are some areas of the Artificial Intelligence field.

Machine learning is one of the known areas in the AI field, where a lot of mathematical models or equations are used for prediction and data analysis.

Deep learning uses machine learning techniques but with large amount of data. For example, if you need to work with data of past ten years and you need your program to respond within one second, deep learning techniques worked efficiently by grouping the data into different levels.

Cognitive Computing is a process to simulate the human thoughts with different mathematical models. Cognitive computing works more with complex and nonroutine situations faced by human beings in real-life.

Natural Language Processing (NLP) is another AI area where linguistic and computer science concepts are also merged. Any natural language requires different syntax, semantic and pragmatic rules. NLP techniques allow machines to detect a person's language, process his request and reply to the person automatically. Such example is very common in smart agent application or chatbot you find on some websites.

Computer Vision is about interpreting images. For example, face detection and nose detection applications fall under the computer vision category.

1.5. Programming languages used for AI applications

Today, different programming languages such as Python, Java, visual basic or C++, do have AI functionalities. Most of these languages, require you to have a different set up on your computer, to add these AI functionalities.

The terminology we use in the field of computer science for these group of functionalities, is known as either a package or a library. The latter consists of many modules having different functionalities.

These modules are also known as classes, a term used in Object Oriented Programming (OOP). For more information, the OOP concept is explained in chapter 3 of this book.

The programming language chosen to show AI programs in this book is the Python language.

1.6. Python programming language

Python, a high-level programming language, was designed in 1991 by Guido van Rossum. A high-level programming language consists of alphabetical letters and punctuation marks. A low-level programming language consists of only a series of 0's and 1's, compared to high-level language where the language is human readable.

1.7. Installation steps for AI development

Spyder application has been used to test the different Python codes of this book. This tool comes within the installation of Anaconda application set up. If you are comfortable with other types of AI tool, you are encouraged to use any other. You can also searched for keywords such as "AI online compiler" or "Machine Learning online compiler", to practice the codes.

In case you wish to install the software application on your desktop computer or laptop, you will have to download Anaconda from its official website. Anaconda is an application tool having many artificial intelligence packages. You can connect on anaconda.org website for more information.

To write AI applications, use the Spyder application to write and save your codes, but use the "Anaconda Prompt" to run the codes.

To install any AI packages, use the "Anaconda Powershell Prompt". The following commands have been useful for the installation process:

- ➤ pip install speech_recognition
- ➤ pip install pyttsx3
- ➤ pip install pywhatkit
- ➤ pip install pipwin
- ➤ pipwin install pyaudio

Chapter 2: Procedural Programming

2.1 Introduction

Today, there exist many types of programming. The one that we will be learning about in this chapter is the procedural programming paradigm. The language we shall be using is still the Python programming language.

Object Oriented Programming (OOP) is a second programming paradigm which exists. It is not compulsory to use the OOP concept to build an AI application with an educational purpose in mind. However, industry applications work better with the OOP concepts.

For this book, we have been using the procedural programming paradigm for all the codes. However, AI application, though in the procedural way, relies on a lot of in-built libraries. The latter are built within the OOP model. Understanding how OOP works will help you understand how individual Python libraries or modules work. In chapter 3, more information will be given on OOP model.

2.2. Concepts in computer programming

There are five main concepts in procedural programming: variables, arrays, conditional statements (if-then, else), repetitions, and functions. Other concepts include comments, indentation, pre-built functionalities, algorithm, and concatenation.

Comments: Any descriptive comments can be written in Python by adding the character **#** at the beginning of any line of code.

Indentation: To group codes under a particular concept or section, we often use a series of blank spaces at the start of a line of code. This is known as "indentation."

For example:

def draw():

    print("drawing") #indentation is adding some blank spaces before typing line *print("drawing").* Note that line *def draw()* does not contain any blank space.

Pre-built functionalities: Python provides in-built functionalities (i.e., libraries) that can be imported using the keyword "import."

Algorithm: Before writing codes, the programming logic can be written in the English language to detail out the different steps in sequential order.

Concatenation: is a process where you can add at most two words together to form a single word (two set of characters "Tues" and "Day", when concatenated become one single word "TuesDay").

Variables

Variables are the unique identifiers given to a program. Each of them is defined by a unique name. A variable contains one value at a time. Integer and string, two datatypes, are two examples that define the type of value of a variable.

For example, **a="5"**, where **a** is a variable name in Python and the value of variable **a** is "5". In Python, when a value is in either double or single quotes, it is a text character (i.e., a String type). If variable **a** was declared without quotes, as in **a=5**, the value 5, becomes an integer value.

Arrays

An array is a variable that can contain more than one value in a program.

For example: a= [4,5,6,7]

The above statement shows that array **a** contains four values: 4,5,6, and 7.

Conditional statements

Conditional statements are important in any program because they define the true and false possibility of an event. For example, if you want to go to Ballarat city from Melbourne, the feasible option you may have is to either opt for a car or a train. Conditional statements with "if" and "else" statements allow you to write this code logic in your program. If a car is available for you, you will use "if statement" in your program. If no car is available for you, you will use the "else" part of your statement, indicating you would rather take a train to go to the city.

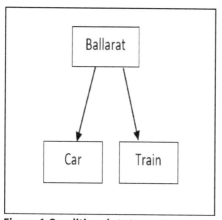

Figure 1 Conditional statements

Python codes:

```
a="car"
if a=="car": #if variable a is equal to "car" value, then
program goes inside the block
    print("Ballarat by car")
else: # if no car is available, train is taken
    print ("Ballarat by train")
```

Figure 2 if-else statements

Repetitions or Iterations

Iterations or repetitions are also known as loops or cycles. If you wish to read the different values of an array, you may use either a "for loop" or a "while loop" to achieve this.

Example 1 with a "for loop":

Refer to the following Figure 3, for explanation which follows.

```
marks=[34,5,95,34]
for i in marks:
    if i>90: # if marks from the array list is greater than 90
        print(i) # then print the corresponding mark greater
than 90
```

Figure 3 for loop codes

If you expect a program to display the marks which are greater than 90 on the screen, you can write the following program:

In the above example, the different marks are stored in the array **marks** with the following values: 34,5,95, 34.

The statement "for i in marks:" will start a looping process. The array "marks" will be reading, one value at a time. Each value from the array will be assigned to the variable "i". In the first loop, the variable "i" will contain value 34. In the second loop, the variable "i", will contain the value 5. In the third loop, the variable "i" will contain the value 95, and in the fourth loop, the variable "i" will contain the value 34.

On each loop, there will be a conditional statement, verifying if the value of the mark is greater than 90. In the third loop, the condition is matched as mark "95" is greater than 90. Among the four given marks (34,5,95, and 34) in the array **marks**, only value **95** met the condition of **if i>90** and **95** is displayed on the screen.

In Python, the "for loop" can be expressed differently to the one shown previously. Instead of having "for i in marks" where variable **i** in each loop is storing the **actual marks** from the array, we could have alternatively written "for i in range(len(marks)):". Here, variable **i**, in each loop, will store the **position number** 0,1,2 or 3 for the corresponding marks of 34,5,95, and 34. "len(marks)" gives us the number of elements (i.e., count) in the array "marks" which is count=4. Storing the position number instead of the actual value implies a change in the line "print(i)", as variable **i** is no longer storing the actual value of the array list. "print(i)" will change to "print(marks[i])"

Example 2 with a "while loop":

The same program as in Example 1, was written this time with a "while loop" in Example 2:

```
marks=[34,5,95,34]
i=0
while i< len(marks):
    if marks[i]>90:
        print(marks[i])  # is executed only if condition is met
    i=i+1 #is executed after if logic
```

Figure 4 while loop codes

The difference between a "while loop" and a "for loop" is that the "while loop" allows more flexibility to skip elements in your array according to your choice. For example, you can have conditions that will either skip by one element (i.e. i=i+1) or in other cases, by two elements (i.e. i=i+2). In a "for loop", everything is restricted on one single line, e.g., "for i in range(len(marks)):". With a for loop, you cannot change the sequence of execution.

Functions

Function is a concept in programming that allows you to reuse your codes at a different point in time in your program. Functions also allow you to structure your codes for a better visual representation.

For example, if you want to use different arrays to validate the different marks, you can use a function to structure your common codes and then reuse the same function each time you need to verify the highest mark with a different list.

```
def func_marks(marks): #grouping of codes
    for i in marks:
        if i>90:
            print(i)


marks=[34,5,95,34] # first array
func_marks(marks) #calling the function with first list
marks=[60,87,98] # second array
func_marks(marks) # calling the same function with a second list
```

Figure 5 function example

The above codes will print value 95 and 98 respectively on the user screen.

Function **func_marks** has been reused twice in the program. As you can see, the same code logic to check the marks, was not duplicated. To achieve this, two different arrays with two different sets of values were used as parameters or arguments to the function.

Chapter 3: Object-Oriented Programming (OOP)

3.1. Introduction

In chapter 2, we have learnt how to program with procedural programming in Python. In chapter 3, you will still be using the basic concepts of variables, values, arrays, loops, conditional statements and functions , but with a different approach, which is the Object-Oriented programming (OOP).

In procedural programming, you design and write your codes in sequential order. In procedural programming, you use the function concept to group operations. However, in OOP, you can group these individual functions to have a user-perspective hierarchical representation of these operations with their individual elements.

For example, if you want to output the sum of two integers inputted by a user, in procedural programming, you do not think about the user as an entity in your codes, but only his operations (actions). In OOP, you think about grouping all the operations in one single area, with a user-perspective in terms of software usage and code maintenance for the developer.

To code in Object-Oriented programming, follow the following two phases as a good practice. Each of these two phases, consists of a series of steps.

The first phase, Phase 1, consists of building the class structure and the second phase, Phase 2, consists of running the class structure with data. For example, the class structure is the "person" and the data to pass to the class, consist of first name, last name and age of the person. Different persons have different names. Hence, their data values differ, but they have the same class structure (categorical or hierarchical structure).

The Phase 1 and Phase 2 steps are listed below. The detail explanation will be given in the next two sections of the book.

Five steps of Phase 1:

- ➢ Step 1: is to build the skeleton of the class.
- ➢ Step 2: create the class constructor.
- ➢ Step 3: is to identify the class's properties.
- ➢ Step 4: Identify the class's behaviours.
- ➢ Step 5: identify the code logic to implement.

Two steps of Phase 2:

- ➢ Step 1: Instantiate the class to create object.
- ➢ Step 2: Perform an action.

3.2. Phase 1

Phase 1 is about building the hierarchical category. In Object-Oriented Programming (OOP), the technical word to define a "hierarchical category" is known as a "class", specifically a parent or subclass.

A "person" can be considered as a class in Object-Oriented programming, and we will call it, a class person. A person normally has some properties such as a first name, a last name, an age, number of eyes, height etc. A person can also have some behaviours such as talking, sleeping, drinking water.

We will follow the following five steps in Phase 1, to build the class for person.

Step 1: is to build the skeleton of the class.

Step 1 is shown in the codes below. The class "Person" has been written as "class Person:" in Python. "pass" is used when you do not want to add any codes in your Python Program, but still want to execute the codes. In this case, no error will be detected as the syntax is recognised by the Python compiler.

```
class Person:

    pass
```

Figure 6 First step of Phase 1

Step 2: create the class constructor

In step two, add the constructor with the following line of codes
"def __init__(self):"

```
class Person:


    def __init__(self):

        pass

```

Figure 7 Second step of Phase 1

Step 3: is to identify the class's properties

In step three, add some other codes to take the first name, last name and age values, as three parameters to the constructor. They can be seen as "self,fname,lname,age" to the constructor "__init__". These values need to be stored in class variables of the class Person. This is achieved with the following codes:

```
    self.firstname=fname
    self.lastname=lname
    self.age=age
```

25

self.firstname, self.lastname and self.age are class variables of the class Person. To note, the keyword "self" in Python, refers to "the current or this class". By default, "self" is needed as one parameter (argument) in the constructor.

The whole code snippets are found below:

```
class Person:

    def __init__(self, fname,lname,age):
        self.firstname=fname
        self.lastname=lname
        self.age=age

```

Figure 8 Third step of Phase 1

Step 4: Identify the class's behaviours

The following codes show the behaviours, also known as the method of the class Person. "displayname" is a method of the class and it is an operation for the class Person. In its operation, it will display the first name and last name of the person.

```
class Person:

    def __init__(self, fname,lname,age):
        self.firstname=fname
        self.lastname=lname
        self.age=lname


    def displayname(self):
        print ("first name is ",self.firstname)
        print ("Last name is ", self.lastname)
```

Figure 9 Fourth step of Phase 1

Step 5: identify the code logic to implement

The codes to print the first name and last name have been implemented within the method "displayname" in step 5 as shown below. This is the goal of the method to print the names on screen and it has been implemented.

In this example, only one method has been shown. However, any number of methods needed by a program can be identified and codes can be implemented accordingly.

```
class Person:

    def __init__(self, fname,lname,age):
        self.firstname=fname
        self.lastname=lname
        self.age=lname

    def displayname(self):
        print ("first name is ",self.firstname)
        print ("Last name is ", self.lastname)
```

Figure 10 Fifth step of Phase 1

3.3. Phase 2

There are two steps in phase 2 and they will be shown in the next two sections.

Step 1: Instantiate the class to create object

The first step of Phase 2 is to run the structure with the different values "John", "Rama" and "12". "John" is the first name, "Rama" is the last name and "12" is the age of the person.

The first object "P1" is created and the term we use is called instantiation. This step is done with the following codes:
p1=Person("John","Rama",12)

```
class Person:
    def __init__(self, fname,lname,age):
        self.firstname=fname
        self.lastname=lname
        self.age=lname
    def displayname(self):
        print ("first name is ",self.firstname)
        print ("Last name is ", self.lastname)
p1=Person("John","Rama",12) #instantiate an object p1 for class
Person
```

Figure 11 First step of Phase 2

If a second Person object, needs to be created with different values, it can be created with the same Person structure as with the following codes:

```
P2=Person("Anie","Rita",39)
```

Step 2: Perform an action

The person object (P1) wants to display its first name and last name on the screen with the method "displayname".

This is achieved by running the following codes:

```
p1.displayname() # perform an action to display names
```

```
class Person:
    def __init__(self, fname,lname,age):
        self.firstname=fname
        self.lastname=lname
        self.age=lname
    def displayname(self):
        print ("first name is ",self.firstname)
        print ("Last name is ", self.lastname)
p1=Person("John","Rama",12) #instantiate an object p1 for class
Person
p1.displayname() # perform an action to display names
```

Figure 12 Second step of Phase 2

After executing the codes in Figure 12, the following outputs are seen on the screen to the user:

first name is John

Last name is Rama

Chapter 4: Building the AI Chatbot

As an overview, the aim is of this book is to build an AI chatbot with different features. The AI chatbot shall be presented to a user with a menu. A user shall be able to interact with the AI chatbot either by typing text or by speaking to the AI chatbot. The upcoming chapters from 5-14, will incrementally add new functionalities to the existing chatbot build. In chapter 15, you will be presented with the compiled codes used for running the AI chatbot.

Facial detection, GPS, Natural Language Processing (NLP) concepts have been used.

Chapter 5: Face Detection

As a first step, for a user to successfully interact with the Chatbot, he should be identified as a human being. In this chapter, the user's face will be detected at the login stage.

To ensure that the user's face is detected prior to log into the Chatbot application, the face detection codes have been implemented as shown below.

```
#import packages
import pandas as pd
import numpy as np


# used for face detection
import cv2


def func_facedetect():


    #import cascade files
    vfaceCascade                                              =
cv2.CascadeClassifier('haarcascade_frontalface_default.xml')


    #video capture
```

```python
vvideo = cv2.VideoCapture(0)


#keep track of the number of faces detected
vcount=0
while True:
    #capture image in a loop
    vret, vimg = vvideo.read()


    #check if face detected
    vfaces = vfaceCascade.detectMultiScale(
        image = vimg,
        scaleFactor=1.1,
        minNeighbors=5


    )


    #count the number of faces detected
    vcount=len(vfaces)


    # if vcount greater than 0, this means one face detected
    if vcount>0:
        break


    #otherwise, keep checking
```

```
    for (x,y,w,h) in vfaces:

        cv2.rectangle(vimg, (x, y), (x+w, y+h), (255, 0, 0), 2)



    #show window for user to see
    cv2.imshow('video camera',vimg)


    #in case user wish to exit the window
    k = cv2.waitKey(30) & 0xff


    # press 'ESC' to exit
    if k == 27:
        break


#release from memory
cv2.destroyAllWindows()


return vcount

func_facedetect() # call face detection function
```

Figure 13 Face detection prior to login

The following eleven steps are required to complete the "func_facedetect"
function:

Step 1: import module cv2 from OpenCV library

```
import cv2
```

Step 2: use an xml cascade file to detect frontal images. The file can be downloaded online.

```
vfaceCascade = cv2.CascadeClassifier('haarcascade_frontalface_default.xml')
```

Step 3: create an object for the video capture to run. The cv2 module has a method "VideoCapture" and a value "0" is passed to the method. This will launch the video camera.

```
vvideo = cv2.VideoCapture(0)
```

Step 4: Check if a face is detected while reading the video camera.

```
vfaces = vfaceCascade.detectMultiScale(
        image = vimg,
        scaleFactor=1.1,
        minNeighbors=5

    )
```

Step 5: count the number of faces detected with "vcount".

```
vcount=len(vfaces)
```

Step 6: if at least one face is detected, exit the face detection process and close the video camera.

```
if vcount>0:
    break
```

Step 7: Otherwise, if no face is detected, keep checking for a face to be detected.

```
#otherwise, keep checking
    for (x,y,w,h) in vfaces:
        cv2.rectangle(vimg, (x, y), (x+w, y+h), (255, 0, 0), 2)
```

Step 8: The codes in step 4 to 7, have been included inside a loop to keep checking until either a face has been detected automatically or when the user himself wishes to exit the facial detection process.

```
while True:
```

Step 9: To exit the window in opencv, the number 27 is required, and the following codes will return the key value you have pressed on the keyboard.

```
vexitkey = cv2.waitKey(30) & 0xff
```

Step 10: At the end of the program, releasing the video object from memory to free up memory by destroying all opened windows.

```
cv2.destroyAllWindows()
```

Step 11: call the "func_facedetect" function.

The function "func_facedetect" can be called at any time in the program whenever it is needed.

```
func_facedetect() # call face detection function
```

Chapter 6: Create a User Menu

A menu is created for a user to interact with the Chatbot application. The different codes logic will be shown in this chapter.

The following six steps have been used to enable a user to interact with a menu.

Step 1: The menu is created in function "func_chatmode". Four options are displayed to a user. The latter is expected to type one digit at a time, to navigate through the different menu options.

The first choice option enables the user to chat with the Chatbot by sending textual messages. The given menu display for this task is "1. Chat with text".

The second choice "2. Chat with Voice", enables a user to speak to the Chatbot for interaction.

The third option "3. Visit Australia with GPS", allows the user to type the location he wishes to depart from and to input a list of preferred destinations. The AI chatbot will look for a destination which has the shortest distance from the origin and locate the destination on Google Maps.

The last menu option is to exit the program with option 4,

"4. Exit chat".

```
def func_chatmode():

        print("\n\n","*********************************************
        ********************")
            print("  1.Chat with text")
            print("  2.Chat with Voice")
            print("  3.Visit Australia with GPS")
            print("  4.Exit chat")

        print("*****************************************************
        ***************")
```

Step 2: The face detection function is called prior to the menu with the following codes:

```
vret=0

while vret==0:

    func_mainmenu() #call main menu

    vret=func_facedetect() # call face detection function

    if vret==1:

        print("face detected successfully")  #user is a person
```

```
        break

    else:

        print("Face not detected!Please, try again!") #user not recognised
```

A variable "vret" is initialised with value zero at the start of the program. If a face is detected, the value of the variable will change to 1. This new value is caught by calling the function "func_detect()", which returns 1 if a face is detected or a 0 if the face has not been detected. This is shown below:

```
vret=func_facedetect()
```

Step 3: call menu options only if a face has been detected. The function "func_mode" is called only when "vret" variable holds a value of 1.

```
#building the menu for the user

if vret==1:

    vopt=0

    while vopt!=4:

        func_chatmode()
```

Step 4: User chooses menu option 1.

The option chosen by the user is held in variable "vopt". When user chooses option 1, he will be required to send text messages to the Chatbot by using a computer keyboard.

In this case, the Chatbot will reply with the following message:
Chatbot:Hi, hope you are doing good!")

User will be prompted to input the different keywords which he wants to search. In case, he wants to exit from the searching process, he can type "X". A while loop allows the user to input as many keywords as he wishes, as long as no "X" is input:

while v_keywords!="X":

Every time a user inputs a keyword, the latter is stored in an array "arr_list" with the command "arr_list.append(v_keywords)".

After exiting the while loop, the whole list of values in "arr_list" will be passed to a function "func_nlp" to perform a comparison with existing list of values: 'Melbourne museum.','Melbourne Maritime Museum', 'Melbourne Museum of Printing'. The matching processes will be covered in chapter 7. The Count Vectorizer technique has been used to perform the matching at this level.

In case, there is no match of the keywords typed, with the existing values from the program, the user is prompted to input again a set of different keywords. This is why the values for variables "v_keywords" and "arr_count" have been reset at the end of the "if vopt==1:" block.

The following codes show the result of step 4:

```
if vopt==1: #search by text
        print("Chatbot:Hi, hope you are doing good!")
        print("Input different keywords, press X when done!")
        while v_keywords!="X":
          arr_count=arr_count+1
          vtext="Keyword "+str(arr_count)+":"
          v_keywords=input(vtext)
          arr_list.append(v_keywords)

        func_nlp(arr_list)
        v_keywords=""
        arr_count=0
```

Step 5: When user chooses menu option 2, the function "func_voice" is called. He will be allowed to interact with the Chatbot by the help of a microphone.

```
if vopt==2: #search keyword by voice
        func_voice()
```

Step 6: When a user chooses menu option 3, the function "func_inputrange()" of the file gps_codes.py is being called.

```
if vopt==3: # search gps location

        gps.func_inputrange()
```

The file "gps_codes.py" has been imported in the current file and an alias "gps" has been used in the current file.

The file "gps_codes.py" contains all the codes for speech processing and this will be explained later in Chapter 10, which is about chatting with voice.

The full codes are found in the next figure:

```
#menu call
#return value of function, used by many functions


def func_chatmode():


print("\n\n","*********************************************
********************")
    print(" 1.Chat with text")
    print(" 2.Chat with Voice")
    print(" 3.Visit Australia with GPS")
```

```python
    print("  4.Exit chat")

    print("*******************************************************************")

    vret=0

    while vret==0:
        func_mainmenu() #call main menu
        vret=func_facedetect() # call face detection function
        if vret==1:
            print("face detected successfully") #user is a person
            break
        else:
            print("Face not detected!Please, try again!") #user not
recognised

    #building the menu for the user
    if vret==1:
        vopt=0
        while vopt!=4:
            func_chatmode()
            vopt=int(input("Enter option:"))
            if vopt==1: #search by text
```

```
        print("Chatbot:Hi, hope you are doing good!")
        print("Input different keywords, press X when done!")
        while v_keywords!="X":
            arr_count=arr_count+1
            vtext="Keyword "+str(arr_count)+":"
            v_keywords=input(vtext)
            arr_list.append(v_keywords)


        func_nlp(arr_list)
        v_keywords=""
        arr_count=0
    if vopt==2: #search keyword by voice
        func_voice()


    if vopt==3: # search gps location
        gps.func_inputrange()


print ("Program terminated!")
```

Figure 14 Create a picture

Chapter 7: Compare with Count Vectorizer (NLP)

Count vectorizer is a technique in Natural Language Processing (NPL) when it comes to comparing textual characters. In this book, the "Countvectorizer" module from the Python package "sklearn" has been used.

Both menu option 1 and menu option 2, use the "Countvectorizer" module to check the validity of the keyword inputted by the user. In menu option 1, the user will type the keyword and in the case of menu option 2, the user will speak through a microphone to pass the keyword to the "Countvectorizer" module.

You can see the function "func_nlp" is being used twice in the codes.

For menu option 1, arr_list containing the list of values typed by the user is passed to the function "func_nlp" as shown below:

```
func_nlp(arr_list)
```

For menu option 2, in the function "func_voice()", the function "func_nlp" is being called by passing the list of values spoken by the user. The following codes show the list "arr_list" being passed to function "func_nlp".

vcheck=func_nlp(arr_list)

The following figure shows the codes for function "func_nlp". The steps are explained hereafter.

```
#check similar words
test_data    =    ['Melbourne    museum.','Melbourne    Maritime
Museum','Melbourne Museum of Printing']
def func_nlp(vmessage):
   # set of data to be trained by the application


   train_data=vmessage


   # create an object to split the nouns from the train_data list
   vcountvectorizer    =    CountVectorizer(analyzer=    'word',
stop_words='english')


   # get the number of columns
   vcount_column = vcountvectorizer.fit_transform(train_data)


   # get the list of nouns detected
   vcount_tokens = vcountvectorizer.get_feature_names_out ()

```

```
# pass the test_data to the model vcountvectorizer
occurences = vcountvectorizer.transform(test_data)



#display the number of occurences of the different nouns detected
count=0
for word in vcountvectorizer.get_feature_names_out ():


    number=(occurences.toarray().sum(axis=0))[count]
    print("Number of occurences for '", word,"' is ", number)
    count=count+1

r=0
c=0
columncount=len(vcountvectorizer.get_feature_names_out ())
rval=""
for j in occurences.toarray():
  sum1=0
  for c in range(columncount):
   if j[c]==1:
     #print("val",i,j[c],j[c])
     sum1=sum1+1

  if sum1==columncount:
```

```
        print("\n","--------------------------------------------------
")
        print("Chatbot:",test_data[r], "was identified.")


        rval=rval+test_data[r]


        break
    r=r+1
  d.func_userinterface(rval)
  return rval
```

Figure 15 Compare text with Count Vectorizer (NLP)

The following six steps are required to compare text with the Count Vectorizer technique.

Step 1: Identify your tested data and trained data.

The keywords inputted by the user are new to the chatbot and therefore, they need to be trained. In this case, the list inputted by the user, will be passed by value in the array list "vmessage". The latter is assigned to array "train_data" in function "func_nlp" with the code:

train_data=vmessage

The values which are known to your chatbot will be the tested values. The keywords inputted by the user will be tested on these known values. The latter have been pre-defined in the Python codes. The array list "test_data" contains these known values. Melbourne museum, Melbourne Maritime Museum and Melbourne Museum of Printing have been added to the array list "test_data".

The values inputted by the user either via keyboard or microphone, will be compared with these three values.

```
test_data = ['Melbourne museum.','Melbourne Maritime Museum','Melbourne Museum of Printing']
```

Step 2: Create a grammatical schema for the keywords inputted by the user. As we need to search for these keywords, we will have to base our schema from them. This is achieved by using the CountVectorizer function from Python sklearnlibrary.

```
vcountvectorizer = CountVectorizer(analyzer= 'word', stop_words='english')
```

Step 3: Identify number of columns in your schema.

```
vcount_column = vcountvectorizer.fit_transform(train_data)
```

Step 4: Identify number of words which need to be trained.

```
vcount_tokens = vcountvectorizer.get_feature_names_out ()
```

vcount_column and vcount_tokens should normally contain same values.

Step 5: Get the number of occurrences of each word detected (column) in the schema. Step 5 has been done to verify the maximum occurrences of each word after performing comparison between the train_data and test_data list of values. This was important for us to check if step 6 is correct. The same number of occurrences should be fetched in step 6.

```
occurences = vcountvectorizer.transform(test_data)
count=0
for word in vcountvectorizer.get_feature_names_out ():

        number=(occurences.toarray().sum(axis=0))[count]
        # print("Number of occurences for '", word,"' is ", number)
        count=count+1
```

Step 6: Every value in test_data array is now read on each row of a matrix and every values in the train_data are the column headers of the matrix.
For each value recognised by the chatbot in the test_data list,
```
for j in occurences.toarray():
```
, identify the header column with

```
for c in range(columncount):
```

Every time, a column header (keyword search) has a match in one of the row values (list of test_data) in the matrix, the value of 1 is marked in the matrix. The total sum per column header determines the frequency of each keyword searched by the user. The sum is calculated as shown:

```
suml=suml+l
```

Return a message to user if a match is found:

```
if suml==columncount:
    print("\n","-------------------------------------------------------")
    print("Chatbot:",test_data[r], "was identified.")
```

if no match is found, an empty value is sent to the user. The value is tracked with the variable "rval".

If the keywords inputted do not have any match from the content of the existing list (test_data list), user will be prompted to search for a different set of keywords. However, if a similarity has been identified between the keywords and the existing list, chatbot will reply to user and acknowledge user that the keywords have been identified and provide user with a description of the more accurate word identified as shown in the previous codes.

Step 7: In this step, the matching words either singular or multiple, are passed to the function "func_userinterface" of the file "description_list.py". The letter "d" has been made an alias to the current .py file for the "description_list.py" file. The latter uses the TF-IDF technique to retrieve definition of matching words from a text file. The TF-IDF technique will be covered in the next chapter. The code is shown below:

```
d.func_userinterface(rval)
```

Chapter 8: Compare with TF-IDF technique (NLP)

Another method to search keyword efficiently in Natural Language Processing (NLP) is the TF-IDF Vectorizer technique. This has been used to extract definition of a particular keyword from a text document.

In this example, we will still be using the Python library "sklearn", but we will import the TfidfVectorizer module this time.

```
import string # to process standard python strings
import nltk
from nltk.stem import WordNetLemmatizer
from sklearn.feature_extraction.text import TfidfVectorizer
from sklearn.metrics.pairwise import cosine_similarity
import warnings
warnings.filterwarnings('ignore')
# Keyword Matching


with open('chatbot_list.txt','r', encoding='utf8', errors ='ignore') as fin:
    raw = fin.read().lower()
```

```
#TOkenisation

sent_tokens = nltk.sent_tokenize(raw)# converts to list of sentences
word_tokens = nltk.word_tokenize(raw)# converts to list of words


# Preprocessing
lemmer = WordNetLemmatizer()
def LemTokens(tokens):
     return [lemmer.lemmatize(token) for token in tokens]
remove_punct_dict  =  dict((ord(punct),  None)  for  punct  in
string.punctuation)
def LemNormalize(text):
     return
LemTokens(nltk.word_tokenize(text.lower().translate(remove_punct_di
ct)))



# Generating response
def func_sendmessage(sentence):
   bot_response=''
   sent_tokens.append(sentence)
   TfidfVec       =       TfidfVectorizer(tokenizer=LemNormalize,
stop_words='english')
```

```
tfidf = TfidfVec.fit_transform(sent_tokens)
vals = cosine_similarity(tfidf[-1], tfidf)
idx=vals.argsort()[0][-2]
flat = vals.flatten()
flat.sort()
req_tfidf = flat[-2]
if(req_tfidf==0):
    return "We are sorry. We cannot understand your question."

else:
    bot_response = bot_response+sent_tokens[idx]
    return bot_response


def func_userinterface(v_chatmessage):

    var_presponse=func_sendmessage(v_chatmessage)
    print("Chatbot:"+var_presponse)
    print("----------------------------------------------------","\n")
```

Figure 16 Convert a text into an image

TfidfVectorizer module will be used to compare the first keyword that has a match with a list of values known by the

Chatbot. A description for this particular keyword is retrieved from a document file (.txt). The codes are displayed in the next figure.

The following nine steps have been taken to retrieve the definition of the keyword which has a first match in the chatbot application:

Step 1: Import the different packages needed for AI functionalities

import string, is used to work with textual information.

import nltk, is used to work with natural language processing to recognise the different message sent by the customer to the chatbot.

from nltk.stem import WordNetLemmatizer, is used to split words into different structures or grammars.

from sklearn.feature_extraction.text import TfidfVectorizer, is used for processing the different grammars efficiently with vectors.

from sklearn.metrics.pairwise import cosine_similarity, is used to compare string with cosine_milarity function.

import warnings, any issue that may not be an error to the chatbot, but to be catered by the technical person. For example, if one of the package is deprecated and the technical person will have to update the package with the latest version.

Step 2: build the content of your text file. It should look like an English dictionary having a set of definition or answers ready to be consumed by the AI chatbot application.

For example, the file "chatbot_list.txt" has the following content:

The Melbourne Museum is a natural and cultural history museum located in the Carlton Gardens in Melbourne, Australia. Located adjacent to the Royal Exhibition Building, the museum was opened in 2000 as a project of the Government of Victoria, on behalf of Museums Victoria which administers the venue. The museum won Best Tourist Attraction at the Australian Tourism Awards in 2011.

Melbourne Museum of Printing (MMOP) is a working museum of typography and printing. Since 1993 the museums focus has been on the retention of traditional printing methods and equipment. Initially established as the Australian Type Company; containing a comprehensive collection of printing presses, typesetting machines, types and other print-related artefacts in addition to its Monotype-based typecasting machines and matrix collection.

> The Melbourne Maritime Museum, managed by the National Trust of Australia, is situated in South Wharf on the Yarra River in the city of Melbourne, Victoria, Australia. It is home to the Polly Woodside Barque, the now restored cargo vessel launched in 1885.

Figure 17 Content of chatbot_list.txt

Step 3: read the content of chatbot_list.txt

```
with open('chatbot_list.txt','r', encoding='utf8', errors ='ignore') as fin:
    raw = fin.read().lower()
```

Step 4: convert all content of the file to lowercase.

```
raw = fin.read().lower()
```

Step 5: convert the list to sentences.

```
sent_tokens = nltk.sent_tokenize(raw)# converts to list of sentences
```

Step 6: convert the list into words.

```
word_tokens = nltk.word_tokenize(raw)# converts to list of words
```

Step 7: use the function WordNetLemmatizer, to work the structure of the different sentences and word from the textfile "chatbot_list.txt".

```
def LemTokens(tokens):
    return [lemmer.lemmatize(token) for token in tokens]
remove_punct_dict = dict((ord(punct), None) for punct in string.punctuation)
def LemNormalize(text):
    return
LemTokens(nltk.word_tokenize(text.lower().translate(remove_punct_dict)))
```

Step 8: upon receiving a message from the customer, the message is split into different structures with the help of function TfidfVectorizer.

```
TfidfVec = TfidfVectorizer(tokenizer=LemNormalize, stop_words='english')
tfidf = TfidfVec.fit_transform(sent_tokens)
```

Step 9: A matching is done with the cosine_similarity function.
```
vals = cosine_similarity(tfidf[-1], tfidf)
```

If no matching is found, an error message "We are sorry. We cannot understand your question." is displayed on the screen. Otherwise, the cosine_similarity function will return the whole sentence where the keyword is identified in the text file.

Function "func_userinterface" has been used as a user interface. It calls the function "func_sendmessage" to perform the verification process for a match.

Outputs on the user's screen:

- ➢ Enter your query here: my debit card is not working.
- ➢ Chelsea: the card is not working, when did it happen?

Chapter 9: Chat with Text (Example)

In this chapter, we will run the program and prompt a user to input different keywords to search by the Chatbot. The user uses his computer keyboard to input the different keywords.

The following codes allow the user to input the different keywords and the function "func_nlp" is called to check for a match.

```
if vopt==1: #search by text
        print("Chatbot:Hi, hope you are doing good!")
        print("Input different keywords, press X when done!")
        while v_keywords!="X":
            arr_count=arr_count+1
            vtext="Keyword "+str(arr_count)+":"
            v_keywords=input(vtext)
            arr_list.append(v_keywords)


            func_nlp(arr_list)
        v_keywords=""
        arr_count=0
```

Figure 18 Input keywords via keyboard

The following result in Figure 19, is seen on the screen when user inputs two keywords, "Melbourne" and "Maritime". The chatbot identified the "Melbourne Maritime Museum" from the three known values it has: Melbourne museum.','Melbourne Maritime Museum','Melbourne Museum of Printing. The "Melbourne Maritime Museum" was identified by the Chatbot with the CountVectorizer technique. Refer to chapter 7, where the program logic for comparison with CountVectorizer module has been explained.

The chatbot further extracted additional information related to the ""Melbourne Maritime Museum" from the document file "chatbot_list.txt" and provide the user with a detail description about the ""Melbourne Maritime Museum".

You can see the following description presented to the user:

The melbourne maritime museum, managed by the national trust of australia, is situated in south wharf on the yarra river in the city of melbourne, victoria, australia.

Figure 19 shows the keywords inputted by the user and the responses from the Chatbot:

```
**************************************************
*
```

1.Chat with text

2.Chat with Voice

3.Visit Australia with GPS

4.Exit chat

****

*

Enter option: 1

Chatbot:Hi, hope you are doing good!

Input different keywords, press X when done!

Keyword 1:Melbourne

Keyword 2:Maritime

Keyword 3:X

Chatbot: Melbourne Maritime Museum was identified.

Chatbot: The melbourne maritime museum, managed by the

national trust of australia, is situated in south wharf on the

yarra river in the city of melbourne, victoria, australia.

****

*

1.Chat with text

2.Chat with Voice

3.Visit Australia with GPS

```
  4.Exit chat

**************************************************

*

Enter option:


```

Figure 19 Output when chatting with text

Chapter 10: Chat with Voice (Example)

The following codes have been used for requesting a user to input different keywords with his microphone. If the user wishes to exit from the input process, he can say "X" and the program will start performing the comparison between the keywords spoken and the known words. If the word cannot be found by the function "func_nlp", the first keyword typed will be searched on "google.com" with the command "pywhatkit.search(arr_list[0])".

```
def func_voice():

    v_keywords=""
    arr_count=0
    print("Chatbot:Hi, hope you are doing good!")
    print("Input with voice different keywords, press X when done!")
    while (v_keywords).upper()!="X":
        arr_count=arr_count+1
        v_keywords = func_speak()
        arr_list.append(v_keywords)


    vcheck=func_nlp(arr_list)
    if vcheck!="":
```

```
    func_speakagent(vcheck)


  else:
    func_speakagent('Sorry, cannot find the word. We will search it
online for you! ')
    pywhatkit.search(arr_list[0])
```

Figure 20 Chat with Voice

The following result is seen on the screen when user says the two words, "Melbourne" and "Printing" to the Chatbot by using a Microphone. The chatbot identified the "Melbourne Museum of Printing" as a match from the three known values it has: 'Melbourne museum.','Melbourne Maritime Museum' and 'Melbourne Museum of Printing'.

The "Melbourne Museum of Printing" was identified having the most similarity to the keywords searched. The Chatbot uses the Count Vectorizer technique to identify this similarity. Refer to chapter 7, where the program logic for comparison has been explained.

The chatbot further extracted additional information with the Tfidtransformer technique to retrieve a description of

"Melbourne Maritime Museum" from the document file "chatbot_list.txt" and provide the user with a the description.

You can see the following description presented to the user:

Melbourne museum of printing (mmop) is a working museum of typography and printing.

```
Please wait for face detection to log into the chat..................
Exit with ESC character
face detected successfully


***************************************************
*
    1.Chat with text
    2.Chat with Voice
    3.Visit Australia with GPS
    4.Exit chat
***************************************************
*
Enter option:2
Chatbot:Hi, hope you are doing good!
Input with voice different keywords, press X when done!
Lisening....
Melbourne
```

```
Lisening....
printing
Lisening....
x


---------------------------------------------------------

Chatbot: Melbourne Museum of Printing was identified.
Chatbot: Melbourne museum of printing (mmop) is a
working museum of typography and printing.

---------------------------------------------------------


*************************************************
*
  1.Chat with text
  2.Chat with Voice
  3.Visit Australia with GPS
  4.Exit chat
*************************************************
*
Enter option:
```

Figure 21 Output when chatting with Voice

Chapter 11: Locate a region with GPS

In this chapter, you will learn how to use the Global Positioning System (GPS) technology to fetch the location of different regions.

In the following example, the city "Adelaide" was passed to the function "func_display" and the program produces a file "map_region.html". The latter encircles the region on Google Maps in online mode. An offline map is also possible if you do not have a Google Maps API key.

```
# use for gps technology in Python
from geopy.geocoders import Nominatim


#use to plot on graph
import gmplot



def func_display(regionname):

    # calling the Nominatim tool
    loc = Nominatim(user_agent="GetLoc")
```

```python
# taking the name of the region
getLoc = loc.geocode(regionname)

# identify latitude
latitude_list =[]
latitude_list.append(getLoc.latitude)

#identify longitude
longitude_list=[]
longitude_list.append(getLoc.longitude)

#plot on the map
gmap = gmplot.GoogleMapPlotter(getLoc.latitude,
                    getLoc.longitude, 13 )

#use color to mark the region
gmap.scatter( latitude_list, longitude_list, 'blue', size = 500, marker
= False)


# outline border

gmap.polygon(latitude_list, longitude_list, color = 'purple')
```

```
#optional for apikey
#if you do not have a key, the map will work offline
#gmap.apikey = "YOUR_GOOGLEMAP_API_KEY"


#draw the map and save to map_region file
gmap.draw( "map_region.html" )



func_display("Adelaide")
```

Figure 22 location with GPS

Adelaide in Australia is encircled in blue color on the file "map_region.html". Due to copy right permission, we are not displaying Google Maps here. However, do open the file "map_region.html" to see the encircled region.

The following steps explain the different codes used to locate a region on a map:

Step 1: pass the name of the region to the function "func_display" in the codes.

```
func_display("Adelaide")
```

Step 2: Get the satellite location of the region and store it in the variable "getLoc".

```
getLoc = loc.geocode(regionname)
```

Step 3: create a list for all your latitude coordinates of the region.

```
latitude_list =[]
```

```
latitude_list.append(getLoc.latitude)
```

Step 4: create a second list for all your longitude coordinates of the region.

```
longitude_list=[]
```

```
longitude_list.append(getLoc.longitude)
```

Step 5: plot the coordinates on the map and enlarge the map with size "13".

```
gmap = gmplot.GoogleMapPlotter(getLoc.latitude,getLoc.longitude, 13 )
```

Step 6: use blue color to encircle the located region. The size of the circle will be 500 px. As we are using circle to mark the region, we will set false to marker property.

#use color to mark the region

```
gmap.scatter( latitude_list, longitude_list, 'blue', size = 500, marker = False)
```

Step 7: Outline the circle with a different color. The purple color has been chosen.

```
gmap.polygon(latitude_list, longitude_list, color = 'purple')
```

Step 8: This step is optional. If you have a google API key for Google Maps, then you may use it in your program. If your main purpose is to learn Google Maps development, you can work without an API key. Otherwise, for any other purposes, it is recommended to have one Google API key.

Look online for the different instructions to register yourself for one of the keys. The steps are pretty easy to follow.

Step 9: Generate an html file with the region encircled.

```
gmap.draw( "map_region.html" )
```

Chapter 12: Distance between two regions

In chapter 11, you have learned how to locate one singular region on a map by retrieving the latitudinal and longitudinal points of the region via GPS.

In this chapter, you will learn how to retrieve latitudinal and longitudinal points of multiple regions. You will then compare each of them with an origin point, having its own latitude and longitude. To retrieve the distance between two points, the Euclidean distance formula has been used. It will be detailed out in the steps sections.

The following codes show the function func_EuclideanDistance for calculating the distance between two regions. The function "func_inputrange" is also shown in the codes to request user to input the origin and the different regions they want to visit.

```
#get the latitude and longitude, return the values to be used
def func_getloc(point):
    loc = Nominatim(user_agent="GetLoc")
    arrl=[]
    # entering the location name
    getLoc = loc.geocode(point)
    latitude_list =[]
```

```
        latitude_list.append(getLoc.latitude)

        longitude_list=[]

        longitude_list.append(getLoc.longitude)

        arrl.append([])

        arrl[0].append(getLoc.latitude)

        arrl[0].append(getLoc.longitude)


        return getLoc,arrl[0][0],arrl[0][1]


    #Euclidean's distance calculation
    def func_EuclideanDistance(point1, point2):
        vdifferences = [point1[x] - point2[x] for x in range(len(point1))]


        #eliminate negative and apply pythagoras theorem
        differences_squared = [(difference ** 2) for difference in vdifferences]


        vsum = sum(differences_squared)
        #print(vsum)
        return math.sqrt(vsum)


    #menu to input the starting point and destinations you wish to go
    def func_inputrange():


        # input starting point


        starting_point=input("From where do you want to start? ")
```

```python
    startp,x1,y1=func_getloc(starting_point)  # return three values from
func_getloc

    #input the number of destinations you want to analyse
    num=int(input("How many destinations you want to travel?")) #

    listdes={}
    listarr={}

    #initialising listdes with empty values
    for i in range(num):
        listdes[i]=""

    #request user to input his destination list
    for i in range(num):
        text=str(i+1)+".To:"
        des=input(text)
        des,x,y=func_getloc(des)
        listdes[i]=des # store string values
        listarr[i]=x,y # store only coordinates for calculation

    count=0 # use to track the number of loops
    checkshortest=10000 #largest value possible
    region="" #the region with shortest distance
```

```
#loop through geolocation for each destination
for city, coord in listdes.items():


  z=x1,y1 # starting points


  #distance calculated from starting points
  distance= func_EuclideanDistance(z, listarr[count])


  #print on screen all the destinations and the distance from origin
  print("\n","----------------------------------------------------")
  print(str(count+1),".", coord," distance is ", distance,".")
  print("----------------------------------------------------","\n")
  count=count+1
```

Figure 23 Distance between two regions

The results are shown here:

```
**************************************************
```

   1.Chat with text

   2.Chat with Voice

   3.Visit Australia with GPS

   4.Exit chat

```
**************************************************
```

Enter option:3

From where do you want to start? Melbourne

How many destinations you want to travel?4

1.To:Perth

2.To:Sydney

3.To:Ballarat

4.To:France

```
--------------------------------------------------
```

1 . Perth, City of Perth, Western Australia, 6000, Australia
distance is 29.68636270549798 .

```
--------------------------------------------------
```

```
--------------------------------------------------
```

2 . Sydney, Council of the City of Sydney, New South Wales,
Australia distance is 7.386450951615921 .

```
--------------------------------------------------
```

```
--------------------------------------------------
```

3 . Ballarat, City of Ballarat, Victoria, 3350, Australia distance is
1.1310079293730797 .

 ----

4 . France distance is 166.1226432542113 .

 ****

   1.Chat with text

   2.Chat with Voice

   3.Visit Australia with GPS

   4.Exit chat

 ****

Enter option:

The following two phases, Phase 1 and Phase 2, have been
covered to achieve the above program:

Phase 1: Euclidean distance

In Phase 1, we will understand the Euclidean formula first.

We will be using an example here between two points (1,2) and
(3,5) so that you can get a better idea how it works, before
getting into the codes for the chatbot.

The Euclidean formula is based on the Pythagoras theorem's formula.

According to the law of Pythagoras Theorem,

$(AB)^2 = (AC)^2 + (BC)^2$

Hence, if we have two sets of coordinates (X1,Y1) and (X2,Y2), using the Pythagoras' formula again, we will result into the following;

$(AB)^2 = (X2-X1)^2 + (Y2-Y1)^2$

Therefore, Euclidean Distance is calculated as the square root of $[(X2-X1)^2 + (Y2-Y1)^2]$.

This Euclidean Distance formula has been applied in Figure 23, to calculate the distance between an origin point, the place where to depart and the destination, the place a user wishes to go.

Six steps have been followed to write the program:

Step 1: define the two points.

vpoint1 = (1,2)

81

vpoint2 = (3,5)

Step 2: For each coordinate points, perform its difference (x1-x2) and (y1-y2).

vdifferences = [point1[x] - point2[x] for x in range(len(point1))]

Step 3: As the differences calculated in Step 2 might be in negative values, the square of both numbers can be done with the following codes:

differences_squared = [(difference ** 2) for difference in vdifferences]

Step 4: the sum of the two values can be calculated with:

vsum = sum(differences_squared)

Step 5: The square root of the final value was done.

math.sqrt(vsum)

Step 6: The distance is printed on screen by calling function "func_EuclideanDistance" with the two points.

```
print("Distance between the two points is ", func_EuclideanDistance(point1,
point2))
```

Phase 2: Input values and calculate distance

In phase 2, we will ask the user to input the origin and the different places he wishes to travel. The distance calculation will be performed for each region input from the origin points.

The following steps will be taken to achieve this.

Step 1: request user to input region to depart from and assign the value to the variable "starting_point".

```
starting_point=input("From where do you want to start? ")
```

Step 2: Get the latitude and longitude of the region to be departed from and assign the values to x1 and y1 respectively.

```
startp,x1,y1=func_getloc(starting_point) # return three values from func_getloc
```

Step 3: Input the number of regions you wish to visit.
```
num=int(input("How many destinations you want to travel?"))
```

$y = 2 * x + 4$

Step 4: Input in words, the different regions you wish to visit.

```
for i in range(num):
        text=str(i+1)+".To:"
        des=input(text)
        des,x,y=func_getloc(des)
        listdes[i]=des # store string values
        listarr[i]=x,y # store only coordinates for calculation
```

Step 5: for every destination you wish to visit, calculate the distance between the origin and the destination.

```
for city, coord in listdes.items():

        z=x1,y1 # starting points
        #distance calculated from starting points
        distance= func_EuclideanDistance(z, listarr[count])
```

Step 6: Print on the screen the distance for each destination from the origin.

```
#print on screen all the destinations and the distance from origin
        print("\n","-----------------------------------------------------")
        print(str(count+1),".", coord," distance is ", distance,".")
        print("-----------------------------------------------------","\n")
```

Chapter 13: Shortest distance to travel

The following set of codes is an extension of the previous chapter. After calculating the distance for each destination, a comparison is done to determine the shortest distance to travel from the origin. This comparison is done with the following codes:

```
if distance<checkshortest:
    checkshortest=distance
    region=coord
```

The variable "region" keeps track of the name of the region with the shortest distance from origin.

At the end of the program, the region with the shortest distance from the origin point, is displayed to the user . For example, the shortest distance from Melbourne is Ballarat, among the region inputted by the user in Chapter 11: Perth, Sydney, Ballarat and France. The codes to detect the smallest distance are shown below. The output to the user's screen is followed.

The codes are shown here:

```
for city, coord in listdes.items():

    z=xl,yl # starting points

    #distance calculated from starting points
    distance= func_EuclideanDistance(z, listarr[count])

    #check shortest distance.
    if distance<checkshortest:
        checkshortest=distance
        region=coord

func_display(region)
    #display name of the region with shortest distance from origin

    print("\n","----------------------------------------------------------")
    print("Shortest Distance is at ",region,'.')
    print("----------------------------------------------------","\n")
```

Figure 24 Shortest distance comparison

Output on the user's screen:

Please wait for face detection to log into the chat..................

Exit with ESC character

face detected successfully

****

  1.Chat with text

  2.Chat with Voice

  3.Visit Australia with GPS

  4.Exit chat

****

Enter option:3

From where do you want to start? Melbourne

How many destinations you want to travel?4

1.To:Perth

2.To:Sydney

3.To:Ballarat

4.To:France

----

1 . Perth, City of Perth, Western Australia, 6000, Australia distance is 29.68636270549798 .

----

2 . Sydney, Council of the City of Sydney, New South Wales, Australia distance is 7.386450951615921 .

----

3 . Ballarat, City of Ballarat, Victoria, 3350, Australia distance is
1.1310079293730797 .

----

4 . France distance is 166.1226432542113 .

Shortest Distance is at Ballarat, City of Ballarat, Victoria, 3350,
Australia .

****

  1.Chat with text

  2.Chat with Voice

  3.Visit Australia with GPS

  4.Exit chat

****

Enter option:

Chapter 14: Plot region on Google Maps

The following values have been tested. User wishes to depart from "Melbourne" and would like to travel to three Australian cities: Perth, Ballarat and Canberra. User also wants to consider options to travel to France.

The chatbot provides user with the shortest distance which is Ballarat City. The latter has been mapped and plotted on Google Maps (open file map_region.html).

Output on the user's screen:

Please wait for face detection to log into the chat...................
Exit with ESC character
face detected successfully

```
***************************************************
  1.Chat with text

  2.Chat with Voice

  3.Visit Australia with GPS

  4.Exit chat
***************************************************
```

Enter option:3

From where do you want to start? Melbourne

How many destinations you want to travel?4

1.To:Perth

2.To:France

3.To:Ballarat

4.To:Canberra

----

1 . Perth, City of Perth, Western Australia, 6000, Australia distance is 29.68636270549798 .

----

2 . France distance is 166.1226432542113 .

----

3 . Ballarat, City of Ballarat, Victoria, 3350, Australia distance is 1.1310079293730797 .

----

4 . Canberra, District of Canberra Central, Australian Capital Territory, 2601, Australia distance is 4.843277748109772 .

Shortest Distance is at Ballarat, City of Ballarat, Victoria, 3350, Australia .

```
**************************************************

   1.Chat with text

   2.Chat with Voice

   3.Visit Australia with GPS

   4.Exit chat

**************************************************
```

Enter option:

Chapter 15: The full AI Chatbot codes

menu_main.py:

```python
# -*- coding: utf-8 -*-
"""
Created on Tue Dec 27 22:26:22 2022

@author: user
"""
#import packages
import pandas as pd
import numpy as np

# used for face detection
import cv2

#used for NLP
#import natural language processing library for extraction
from sklearn.feature_extraction.text import CountVectorizer

#speech processing
import speech_recognition as sr
import pyttsx3
import datetime
import pywhatkit
```

```python
#used for chatbotsearch
import description_list as d
import gps_codes as gps

#used to catch words from user
arr_list=[]
arr_count=0
v_keywords=""

#function to detect face before log into the system
def func_facedetect():

    #import cascade files
    vfaceCascade                                              =
cv2.CascadeClassifier('haarcascade_frontalface_default.xml')

    #video capture
    vvideo = cv2.VideoCapture(0)

    #keep track of the number of faces detected
    vcount=0
    while True:
        #capture image in a loop
        vret, vimg = vvideo.read()
```

```python
#check if face detected
vfaces = vfaceCascade.detectMultiScale(
    image = vimg,
    scaleFactor=1.1,
    minNeighbors=5


)



#count the number of faces detected
vcount=len(vfaces)


# if vcount greater than 0, this means one face detected
if vcount>0:
    break


#otherwise, keep checking
for (x,y,w,h) in vfaces:
    cv2.rectangle(vimg, (x, y), (x+w, y+h), (255, 0, 0), 2)



#show window for user to see
cv2.imshow('video camera',vimg)


#in case user wish to exit the window
k = cv2.waitKey(30) & 0xff
```

```python
    # press 'ESC' to exit
    if k == 27:
        break



  #release from memory
  cv2.destroyAllWindows()


  return vcount

#always call this menu for face detection, this is the main menu
def func_mainmenu():
  print("Please wait for face detection to log into the
chat...................")
  print("Exit with ESC character")



def func_chatmode():


print("\n\n","******************************************
************************")
    print("  1.Chat with text")
    print("  2.Chat with Voice")
    print("  3.Visit Australia with GPS")
    print("  4.Exit chat")
```

```python
print("*********************************************
******************")


#check similar words
test_data = ['Melbourne museum.','Melbourne Maritime
Museum','Melbourne Museum of Printing']
def func_nlp(vmessage):
    # set of data to be trained by the application


    train_data=vmessage


    # create an object to split the nouns from the train_data list
    vcountvectorizer = CountVectorizer(analyzer= 'word',
stop_words='english')

    # get the number of columns
    vcount_column = vcountvectorizer.fit_transform(train_data)

    # get the list of nouns detected
    vcount_tokens = vcountvectorizer.get_feature_names_out ()

    # pass the test_data to the model vcountvectorizer
```

```
occurences = vcountvectorizer.transform(test_data)



  #display the number of occurences of the different nouns
detected
  count=0
  for word in vcountvectorizer.get_feature_names_out ():


      number=(occurences.toarray().sum(axis=0))[count]
      #   print("Number of occurences for '", word,"' is ",
number)
      count=count+1


  #print(occurences.todense())


  r=0
  c=0
  columncount=len(vcountvectorizer.get_feature_names_out
())
  rval=""
  for j in occurences.toarray():
    sum1=0
    for c in range(columncount):
     if j[c]==1:
       #print("val",i,j[c],j[c])
```

```python
        sum1=sum1+1

    if sum1==columncount:
        print("\n","-------------------------------------------------------")
        print("Chatbot:",test_data[r], "was identified.")

        rval=rval+test_data[r]

        break
    r=r+1
  d.func_userinterface(rval)
  return rval


#microphone

listener = sr.Recognizer()
vspeakagent = pyttsx3.init()



#machine responding
def func_speakagent(response):
  vspeakagent.say(response)
  vspeakagent.runAndWait()

#person commanding machine
def func_speak():
```

```
#say something for example "melboune"
vcommand=""
try:
    with sr.Microphone() as source:
        print('Lisening....')
        voice = listener.listen(source)
        vcommand= listener.recognize_google(voice)
        print(vcommand)
        vcommand = vcommand.lower()


except:
    func_speakagent('Cannot recognise voice!')


return  vcommand

#action to be taken based on word heard
def func_voice():

    v_keywords=""
    arr_count=0
    print("Chatbot:Hi, hope you are doing good!")
    print("Input with voice different keywords, press X when
done!")
    while (v_keywords).upper()!="X":
        arr_count=arr_count+1
        v_keywords = func_speak()
```

```python
        arr_list.append(v_keywords)



    vcheck=func_nlp(arr_list)
    if vcheck!="":

        func_speakagent(vcheck)

    else:
        func_speakagent('Sorry, cannot find the word. We will
search it online for you! ')
        pywhatkit.search(arr_list[0])



#menu call
#return value of function, used by many functions
vret=0

while vret==0:
    func_mainmenu() #call main menu
    vret=func_facedetect() # call face detection function
    if vret==1:
        print("face detected successfully")  #user is a person
        break
    else:
```

```
        print("Face not detected!Please, try again!") #user not
recognised


#building the menu for the user
if vret==1:
    vopt=0
    while vopt!=4:
        func_chatmode()
        vopt=int(input("Enter option:"))
        if vopt==1: #search by text
            print("Chatbot:Hi, hope you are doing good!")
            print("Input different keywords, press X when done!")
            while v_keywords!="X":
                arr_count=arr_count+1
                vtext="Keyword "+str(arr_count)+":"
                v_keywords=input(vtext)
                arr_list.append(v_keywords)



            func_nlp(arr_list)
          v_keywords=""
          arr_count=0
      if vopt==2: #search keyword by voice
          func_voice()
```

```python
        if vopt==3: # search gps location
            gps.func_inputrange()


print ("Program terminated!")
```

description_list.py:

```python
# -*- coding: utf-8 -*-
"""
Created on Fri Dec 16 13:16:12 2022

@author: yeehos
"""
import string # to process standard python strings
import nltk
from nltk.stem import WordNetLemmatizer
from sklearn.feature_extraction.text import TfidfVectorizer
from sklearn.metrics.pairwise import cosine_similarity
import warnings
warnings.filterwarnings('ignore')
# Keyword Matching
```

```
with    open('chatbot_list.txt','r',    encoding='utf8',    errors
='ignore') as fin:
    raw = fin.read().lower()


#TOkenisation


sent_tokens  =  nltk.sent_tokenize(raw)#  converts  to  list  of
sentences
word_tokens  =  nltk.word_tokenize(raw)#  converts  to  list  of
words




# Preprocessing
lemmer = WordNetLemmatizer()
def LemTokens(tokens):
    return [lemmer.lemmatize(token) for token in tokens]
remove_punct_dict  =  dict((ord(punct),  None)  for  punct  in
string.punctuation)
def LemNormalize(text):
    return
LemTokens(nltk.word_tokenize(text.lower().translate(remove
_punct_dict)))


# Generating response
```

```python
def func_sendmessage(sentence):
    bot_response=''
    sent_tokens.append(sentence)
    TfidfVec     =     TfidfVectorizer(tokenizer=LemNormalize,
stop_words='english')
    tfidf = TfidfVec.fit_transform(sent_tokens)
    vals = cosine_similarity(tfidf[-1], tfidf)
    idx=vals.argsort()[0][-2]
    flat = vals.flatten()
    flat.sort()
    req_tfidf = flat[-2]
    if(req_tfidf==0):
        return "We are sorry. We cannot understand your
question."

    else:
        bot_response = bot_response+sent_tokens[idx]
        return bot_response



def func_userinterface(v_chatmessage):

    var_presponse=func_sendmessage(v_chatmessage)
    print("Chatbot:"+var_presponse.capitalize())
    print("------------------------------------------------------","\n")
```

gps_codes.py:

```python
# -*- coding: utf-8 -*-
"""
Created on Wed Dec 28 08:12:30 2022

@author: user
"""

# use for gps location, latitude and longitude
from geopy.geocoders import Nominatim

#use to plot on graph
import gmplot

# use to calculate shortest distance
import math


#function to display a blue circle with a purple outline for the
location detected on the map
def func_display(regionname):

    # calling the Nominatim tool
    loc = Nominatim(user_agent="GetLoc")

    # taking the name of the region
```

```python
    getLoc = loc.geocode(regionname)

    # identify latitude
    latitude_list =[]
    latitude_list.append(getLoc.latitude)

    #identify longitude
    longitude_list=[]
    longitude_list.append(getLoc.longitude)

    #plot on the map
    gmap = gmplot.GoogleMapPlotter(getLoc.latitude,
                        getLoc.longitude, 13 )

    #use color to mark the region
    gmap.scatter( latitude_list, longitude_list, 'blue', size = 500,
marker = False)


    # outline border

    gmap.polygon(latitude_list, longitude_list, color = 'purple')

    #optional for apikey
    #if you do not have a key, the program will work offline
    gmap.apikey = "YOUR_GOOGLEMAP_API_KEY"
```

```python
    #draw the map and save to map_region file
    gmap.draw( "map_region.html" )


#get the latitude and longitude, return the values to be used
def func_getloc(point):
    loc = Nominatim(user_agent="GetLoc")
    arr1=[]
    # entering the location name
    getLoc = loc.geocode(point)
    latitude_list =[]
    latitude_list.append(getLoc.latitude)
    longitude_list=[]
    longitude_list.append(getLoc.longitude)
    arr1.append([])
    arr1[0].append(getLoc.latitude)
    arr1[0].append(getLoc.longitude)

    return getLoc,arr1[0][0],arr1[0][1]

#Euclidean's diatnce calculation
def func_EuclideanDistance(point1, point2):
    vdifferences   =   [point1[x]   -   point2[x]   for   x   in
range(len(point1))]
```

```python
    #eliminate negative and apply pythagoras theorem
    differences_squared = [(difference ** 2) for difference in
vdifferences]

    vsum = sum(differences_squared)
    #print(vsum)
    return math.sqrt(vsum)


#menu to input the starting point and destinations you wish to
go
def func_inputrange():

    # input starting point

    starting_point=input("From where do you want to start? ")

    startp,x1,y1=func_getloc(starting_point)  # return three
values from func_getloc

    #input the number of destinations you want to analyse
    num=int(input("How many destinations you want to
travel?")) #

    listdes={}
    listarr={}
```

```python
#initialising listdes with empty values
for i in range(num):
    listdes[i]=""


#request user to input his destination list
for i in range(num):
    text=str(i+1)+".To:"
    des=input(text)
    des,x,y=func_getloc(des)
    listdes[i]=des # store string values
    listarr[i]=x,y # store only coordinates for calculation



count=0 # use to track the number of loops
checkshortest=10000 #largest value possible
region=""  #the region with shortest distance



#loop through geolocation for each destination
for city, coord in listdes.items():

    z=x1,y1 # starting points

    #distance calculated from starting points
    distance= func_EuclideanDistance(z, listarr[count])
```

```
        #check shortest distance.
        if distance<checkshortest:
            checkshortest=distance
            region=coord


    #print on screen all the destinations and the distance from
origin
        print("\n","----------------------------------------------------")
        print(str(count+1),".", coord," distance is ", distance,".")
        print("----------------------------------------------------","\n")
        count=count+1


    #plot the shortest distance on Google Maps
    func_display(region)
    #display name of the region with shortest distance from
origin


    print("\n","----------------------------------------------------")
    print("Shortest Distance is at ",region,'.')
    print("----------------------------------------------------","\n")
```

References

Brown, R. E. (2016). Hebb and Cattell: the genesis of the theory of fluid and crystallized intelligence. *Frontiers in human neuroscience*, *10*, 606.